Motels

American Retro

Motels

American Retro

Travel strengthens America.

U. S. Travel Bureau

Contents

Introduction

"On that road the nation is steadily traveling beyond the troubles of this century, constantly heading toward finer tomorrows. The American Road is paved with hope."

1951 Ford ad

The great highways of America were its very heart and soul. They spanned the limits of this vast country from top to bottom and east to west. They carried the new breed of motorists from good to bad, from boom to bust, through towns with such names as Mammoth Cave, Kentucky; Pleasantville, New York; and Broken Bow, Nebraska; many of them with nothing more than a Main Street and a drugstore.

Along the way these arteries offered succor in the form of welcoming diners, serving plates of wholesome freshly prepared dishes—food that spawned a universal language in the shape of hot dogs, hamburgers, fries, and malts. Comfortable motels with warm rooms offered the latest in modern conveniences, from power showers to the combination television and radio set, and provided a safe haven for the night. They were clean and affordable family businesses, which allowed the nuclear family, for the first time, to explore the wonders of their own land.

Parked outside were the trappings of prosperity—Cadillacs, T-Birds, Chevrolets, and Corvettes—cars that any sane person has always wanted to drive. These were elongated giants, explosions of chrome grilles and wire wheels, creating fantasies of speed and escapism with features taken from aircraft designs and space travel. These were the only beasts capable of taming this extraordinary country, and are as representative of the United States of America as the Statue of Liberty or the Stars and Stripes.

The names of those great roads—Highway 61, Route 66, Pacific 1—have since passed into popular mythology. For those with a passion for adventure, the names evoke images of *Easy Rider*, and the lyrics of Bob Dylan and the Rolling Stones. At the same time, they are able to convey that air of safety and innocence, when mom and pop ushered the kids into the back of the family automobile and headed off on vacation.

Now this golden age is all but gone, although remnants do remain. The highways have fallen into disrepair, superseded by freeways with no recognizable character. Many diners have served their last "special," and a large number of "ma and pa" motels have been swallowed up into chains with such alluring names as Comfort Inn and Motel 6 (we are never told what happened to Motels 1 through 5). Small towns, with the whole of life encapsulated on Main Street, are a far cry from the soulless shopping malls of today. And the cars—oh those glorious, gas-guzzling monsters—have been replaced by sensible, compact, economical models with dull, dull names.

As a tribute to the post-war period when people had money in their pockets and a hankering to spend it, the four titles in the *American Retro* series draw on images, both retro and modern, that resonate with the spirit of '50s America. These pictures are paired with advertising slogans, popular sayings, puns, and quotations from personalities that bring to life an age when being economical with the truth came naturally to the advertisers and salesmen of the day, who were desperate to paint a dazzling and futuristic world in which everyone could share. Motels shamelessly claimed to offer comfort fit for the "Queen of Sheba"; car manufacturers used such buzz words as "Rocket Ride" and "Glamorous new Futuramics"; and diners bedecked themselves in chrome detailing and neon lights.

The *American Retro* series recaptures a little of what made those times so special, with images that will fill those who lived through that age with nostalgia and gently amuse and inform those who did not. Read, remember, and enjoy.

ALO
MOT
POO
MAPLE LEA
GIFTS
T-SHI
MOTEL
HEATED POOL
RECORD
MOTEL
MAPLE LEAF
VACANCY
VACANCY
$39. 1 - 2 PER
TICKET
10 % OFF
VACAN
SPECIAL
FREE
HBO
FREE
ESPN
POOL

Where summer stays and the nation plays.

Kissimmee, Florida

MOONGLO
MOTEL APTS.

NO

When they suggested we

stay at the Wigwam Motel,

I had my reservations.

Wigwam Motel,
Holbrook, Arizona

ROUTE 6
Welcome to KINGMA
CLEAN ROOMS AIRCO

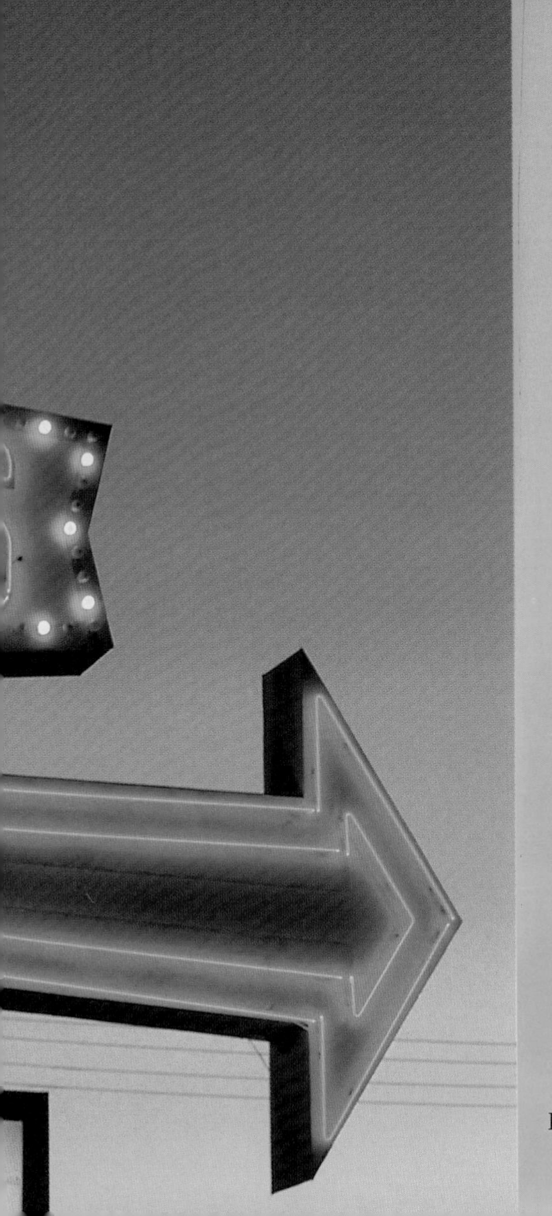

Route 66 is for people who will always be suckers for neon lights

(and home-cooked meals).

Route 66 Motel, Kingman, Arizona

GIFT SHOP
AMERICAN INDIAN
TURQUOISE JEWELRY
FREE TV
VACANCY
SPRINGFIELD NEON
FREE CONTINENTAL BREAKFAST
Plaza Park ESTATES
SPEED LIMIT 35
VISA

Moss
EL
ROUTE
66
OPEN

Hitch your wagon to a star.

Ralph Waldo Emerson

Wagon Wheel Motel,

Cuba, Missouri

WAGON
WHEEL
MOTEL

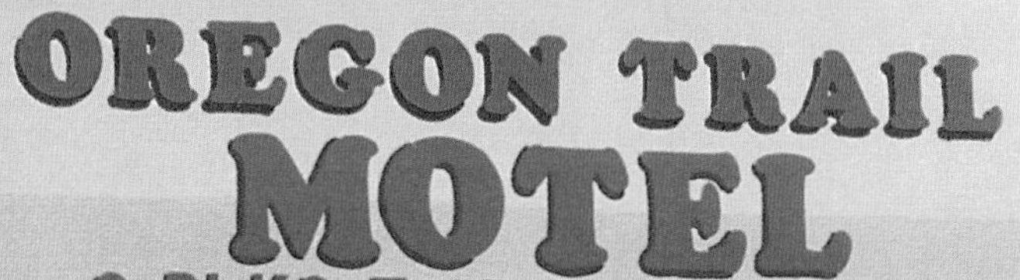
OREGON TRAIL
MOTEL
6 BLKS E. OF 2ND STOP LIGHT
SGL $ 17 95
DBL $ 22 95
& UP
Sensible Rates - Air Conditioned
Phones - Color TV
TRUCK PARKING
PLUG IN
6 BLK. E. OF MAIN ON 26

Go west, young man, go west!

John Babsome Lane Soule

Sign for the Oregon Trail Motel,
Torrington, Wyoming

Oh for a lodge in some vast wilderness,

Some boundless contiguity of shade,

Where rumor of oppression and deceit,

Of unsuccessful or successful war,

Might never reach me more!

William Cowper

Frontier Motel, Cheyenne, Wyoming

ONTIER
OTEL
BUDGET RATES

ON HIGHW
ROUTE U. S. 30
CHEYENN
WYOMING
Ranger
MOTEL

Postcard from
the Ranger Motel,
Cheyenne,Wyoming

I have a dream that one day this nation will rise up, live out the true meaning of its creed: we hold these truths to be self-evident, that all men are equal.

Martin Luther King

Lorraine Motel,
Memphis, Tennessee

MARTIN LUTHER KING JR
JAN 15 1929 — APR 4 1968
FOUNDING PRESIDENT
SOUTHERN CHRISTIAN LEADERSHIP CONFERENCE
THEY SAID ONE TO ANOTHER
BEHOLD HERE COMETH THE DREAMER
LET US SLAY HIM
AND WE SHALL SEE WHAT WILL BECOME OF HIS DREAMS
GENESIS 37 19-20
RALPH DAVID ABERNATHY PRESIDENT

OFFICE
Dr. Wilkinson's
HOT SPRINGS
•Mud
•Steam
•Mineral
BATHS
MASSAGE
COLONICS
PHYSIO THERAPY
DR. JOHN WILKINSON D.C.
OWNER
OPERATOR

With two outdoor warm mineral water pools, and an indoor hydrojet pool open to all guests, Dr. Wilkinson's offers a true spa experience.

Dr. Wilkinson's Hot Springs Motel, Calistoga, California

MOTEL
AAA
Approved
FRESH WATER POOL
ROOMS EFFICIENCIES
VACANCY
Flamingo Inn

Where summer spends the winter.

Marry in haste; repent in Vegas.

Wedding chapel, Las Vegas, Nevada

Cupid's
WEDDING
CHAPEL

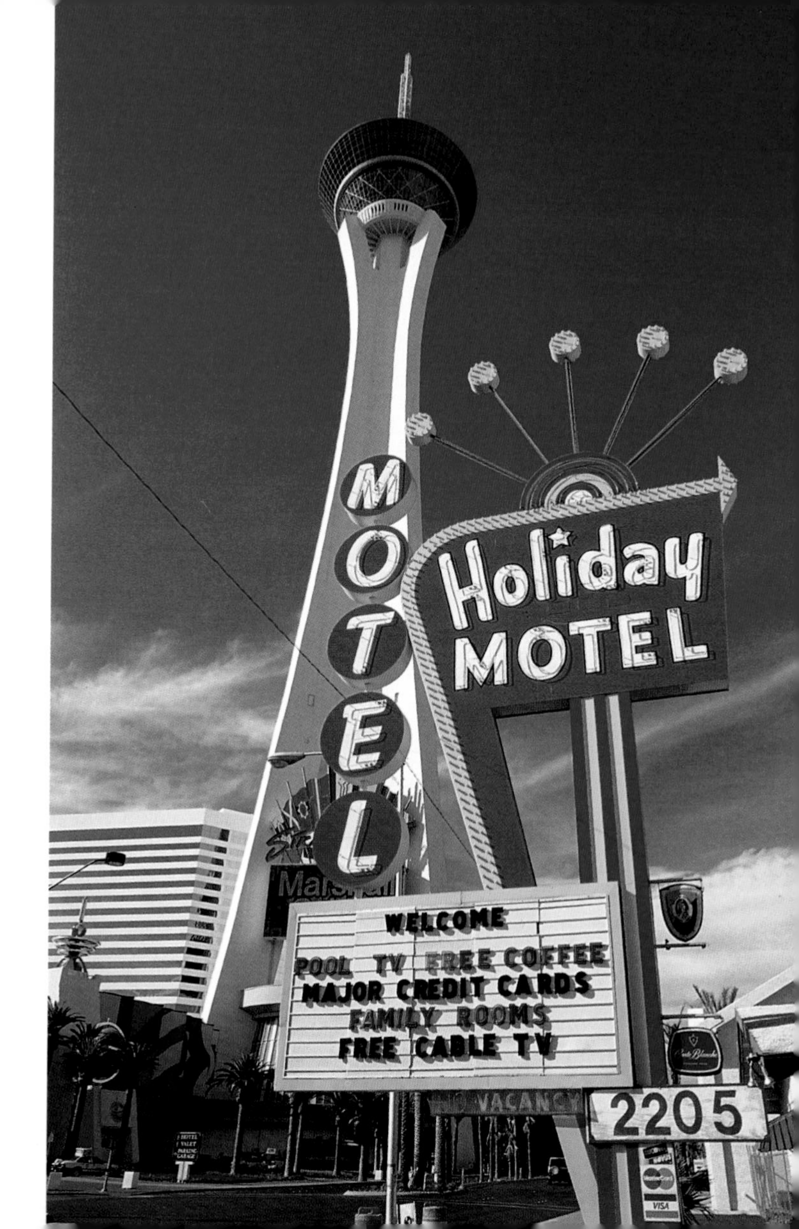
MOTEL
Holiday
MOTEL
WELCOME
POOL TV FREE COFFEE
MAJOR CREDIT CARDS
FAMILY ROOMS
FREE CABLE TV
VACANCY
2205

Escape from the ordinary.

Stratosphere Tower Hotel and Casino on The Strip, Las Vegas, Nevada

A place by the sea.

Bon-Aire on the Sea, Miami Beach, Florida

ON AIRE
B
Bon-Aire
ON THE SEA
Bon-Aire
Bon-Aire

Well, I find that a change of nuisances is as good as a vacation.

David Lloyd George

Approved

Yankee hospitality.

Cold Spring Motel,

Plymouth, Massachusetts

MO

TEL

Oh my America!

my new-found-land.

John Donne

Kelly's Motel,

Key Largo, Florida

KELLY'S
MOTEL
SNORKEL & DIVE
DAY or NIGHT
8:30AM — 1:00 PM — 5:00 PM

OFFICE

Never judge

a summer resort

by its postcards.

Abandoned motel
near Weed, California

Rest your head

at the place

with the headdress.

Chief Motel, near
Joshua Tree National
Monument, California

ROY'S
VACANCY
MOTEL
CAFE

Like all great travelers,

I have seen more than I remember,

and remember more than I have seen.

Benjamin Disraeli

Goose Hunting Capital of the World.

Farris Hotel, Eagle Lake, Texas

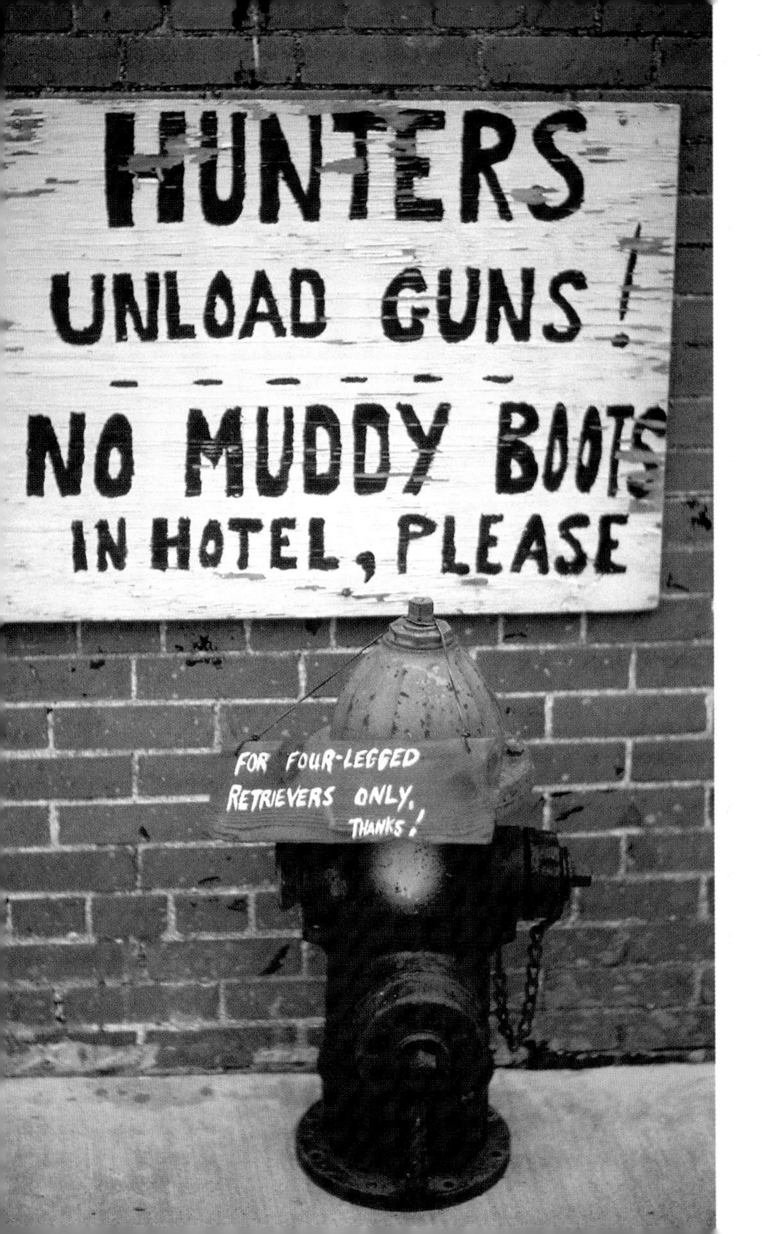
HUNTERS
UNLOAD GUNS!
NO MUDDY BOOTS
IN HOTEL, PLEASE
FOR FOUR-LEGGED
RETRIEVERS ONLY,
THANKS!

With motels,

a bad sign is a bad sign.

Weathered sign

of the Chiriaco Motel

Spend the night, not a fortune.

Motel in Pioche, Nevada

MOTEL

Dream
Inn

From the moment you park your car, you can begin relaxing.

CITY CENTER
226
OFFICE

DTA 203
258·986A

The spa personnel are most attentive to your every need

and are dedicated to making your spa visit a very relaxing and restful time

Dr. Wilkinson's Hot Springs Motel, Calistoga, California

Motel in the
Florida Keys, Florida

LANE
GALLERY
TAXI-18
TEXACO
2966666
CAB
CO.

Santa Fe

is often called

the "City Different."

Loretto Motel,

Santa Fe, New Mexico

You'd be surprised how much it costs to look this cheap.

Dolly Parton

Caesar's Palace and The Mirage Hotel, Las Vegas, Nevada

THE MIRAGE
Kenny & Dolly
NUNN VS STARLING
WORLD MIDDLEWEIGHT CHAMPIONSHIP
APRIL 14TH
NOW APPEARING
Come see our
hite Tigers.
24 hours a
Free Admission
THE MIRAGE
FORUM
CAESARS

Gulf
MO
VACAN

The Sunshine State.

Gulf Side Motel,

Cedar Key, Florida

SMOKY
MOUNTAIN™
MOTOR LODGE™

INFO - EN
TURN
TRY OUR
POSTURE THERMIC
KING WATERBEDS

Wood
HOME FEDERAL
OVERTIME TELLER
Cirrus
VISA
PLUS
OPEN 24 HOURS

HOBO INN
CHARTER·SALES
THE MILWAUKEE ROAD

Nature's paradise,

man's opportunity.

Hobo Inn,

Elbe, Washington

The lobby of some motels

is like God's waiting room.

Cold Spring Motel,
Plymouth, Massachusetts

URANIUM
MOTEL
NO VACANCY
AIR CONDITIONED
4-0375

A helluva place to lose a cow.

Ebenezer Bryce

Sign for the Uranium Motel, Utah

Yeeha!

Lake View Motel, Garden City, Utah

Lake View
CAFE
MOTEL

True comfort

in the cradle

of the revolution.

Peg Leg Motel,
Rockport, Massachusetts

MOTEL PEG LEG

GOLD RUSH INN
MOTEL
NO VACANCY
RESTAURANT · LOUNGE
the Office
COCKTAIL LOUNGE
LICENSED

Gold Rush Inn, Whitehorse, Yukon Territory

Northern exposure.

Town Motel, Gardiner, Montana

TOWN
MOTEL
COLOR
TELEPHONE
AMERICAN EXPRESS

ROXY
PLACE
MOTEL

Friendly, familiar, foreign, and near.

It is an urge, as irresistible as a tide...to travel,

and the ability to travel has forged a united country,

and reduced a vast area to the dimensions of a community.

Swan Hotel, Walt Disney World, Florida

WOODLAND
MOTEL
RESTAURANT
NO VACANCY

Your log cabin away from home.

They appear in early evening

and depart at the first streak of dawn,

and none knows whence or whither.

We only know that they have been.

Budget Inn, Daytona Beach, Florida

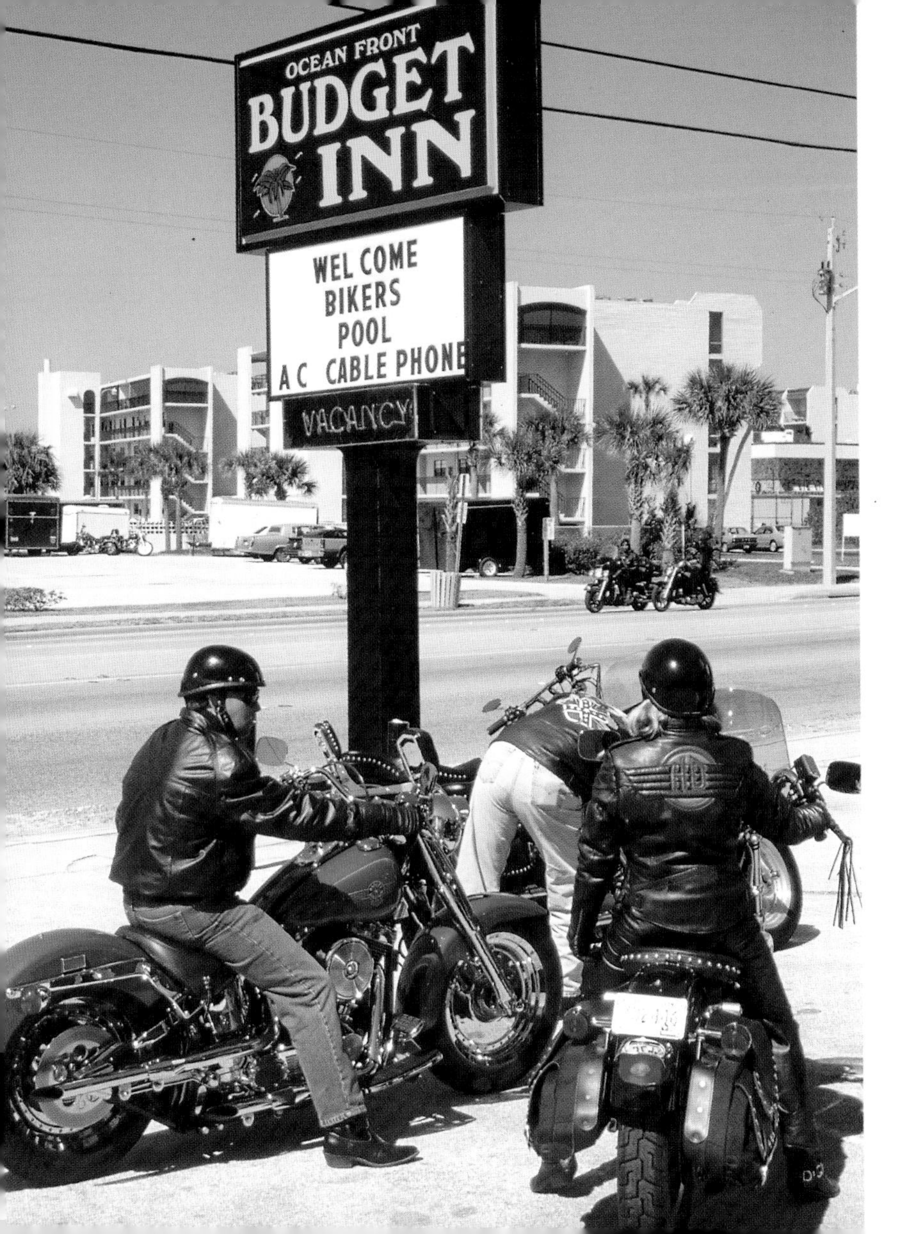
OCEAN FRONT
BUDGET
INN
WEL COME
BIKERS
POOL
A C CABLE PHONE
VACANCY

Smorga Kitchen
FAMILY BUFFET

BUDGET
MOTEL

NO VACANCY
COLOR TV
AIRCONDITIONED
LOW RATES
CLEAN & QUIET
KITCHENETTES

OPEN
FOOD

NO VACANCY
COLOR TV

SPA IN ROOM
FREE
ADULT
Town House
MOTEL
COLOR TV · WATERBEDS ·
AIR COND · WEEKLY RATES ·
rest
OTEL

OF EARTH AND
JUNE 8 AUG 18
IN THE
JUNE 6

Home of the Blues,

birthplace of Rock 'n' Roll.

Lorraine Motel,
Memphis, Tennessee

Wherever you're going, you're sure to find a "B&B" to suit your needs.

MOTEL
AIR CONDITIONED
VACANCY

TV
INDOOR - HOT
MINERAL POOL
OPEN ALL YEAR

OFFICE
UNAUTHORIZED
VEHICLES

The closest I ever got

to a life at sea

was staying in a motel

with a waterbed.

Captain's Bounty Motel,

Rockport, Massachusetts

HISTORIC
ROUTE
66
MOTEL
DIRECT DIAL PHONES
QUEEN BEDS
CABLE T.V. H.B.O.
LARGE FAMILY ROOMS
VACANCY

TEXACO

OK
SALOON
Cocktails
PACKAGE GOODS

Travel strengthens America.

Picture credits

All images reproduced by permission of Corbis Images unless otherwise stated.

Page 8/9: Motel row in Kissimmee, Florida; credit Nik Wheeler.
Page 10/11: Moonglo Motel apartments in Daytona Beach, Florida; credit Lake County Museum.
Page 12/13: Wigwam Motel on Route 66, Holbrook, Arizona; credit Nik Wheeler.
Page 14/15: Route 66 Motel sign in Kingman, Arizona; credit David Paterson.
Page 16/17: Munger Moss Motel along Route 66 in Lebanon, Missouri; reproduced by permission of Travel Ink/Walter Wolfe.
Page 18/19: Wagon Wheel Motel along Route 66 in Cuba, Missouri; reproduced by permission of Travel Ink/Walter Wolfe.
Page 20/21: Sign for the Oregon Trail Motel in Torrington, Wyoming; credit James L. Amos.
Page 22/23: Neon sign for the Frontier Motel in Cheyenne, Wyoming; credit Henry Diltz.
Page 24/25: Postcard from the Ranger Motel in Cheyenne, Wyoming; credit Lake County Museum.
Page 26/27: Lorraine Motel in Memphis, Tennessee; credit Jan Butchofsky-Houser.
Page 28/29: Dr. Wilkinson's Hot Springs Motel in Calistoga, California; credit Robert Holmes.
Page 30/31: Flamingo Inn in Key West, Florida; credit Morton Beebe.
Page 32/33: Wedding chapel in Las Vegas, Nevada; reproduced by permission Travel Ink/Simon Reddy.
Page 34/35: Stratosphere Tower Hotel and Casino in Las Vegas, Nevada; reproduced by permission Travel Ink/Simon Reddy.
Page 36/37: Bon-Aire on the Sea in Miami Beach, Florida; credit Bettmann.
Page 38/39: Dumont combination television and radio set; credit Bettmann.
Page 40/41: Cold Spring Motel in Plymouth, Massachusetts; credit Kevin Fleming.
Page 42/43: Motel on Interstate 90; credit Raymond Gehman.
Page 44/45: Kelly's Motel in Key Largo, Florida; credit Tony Arruza.
Page 46/47: Abandoned motel near Weed, California; credit Bob Rowan.
Page 48/49: Sign for the Chief Motel near Joshua Tree National Monument, California; credit Henry Diltz.
Page 50/51: Roy's Motel and Café along Route 66, California; credit Nik Wheeler.
Page 52/53: Sign on the Farris Hotel in Eagle Lake, Texas; credit Peter Johnson.
Page 54/55: Sign for the Chiriaco Motel; credit Henry Diltz.

Page 56/57: Motel in Pioche, Nevada; credit Gary Thomas Sutto.
Page 58/59: Sign for the Dream Inn in Daytona Beach, Florida; credit Tony Arruza.
Page 60/61: City Center Motel in Seattle, Washington; credit Ray Krantz.
Page 62/63: Dr. Wilkinson's Hot Springs Motel in Calistoga, California; credit Robert Holmes.
Page 64/65: Motel in the Florida Keys, Florida; reproduced by permission of Travel Ink/Abbie Enock.
Page 66/67: Loretto Motel in Santa Fe, New Mexico; credit Craig Lovell.
Page 68/69: Caesar's Palace and the Mirage Hotel in Las Vegas, Nevada; reproduced by permission of Travel Ink/Walter Wolfe.
Page 70/71: Forum of Caesar's Palace in Las Vegas, Nevada; reproduced by permission of Travel Ink/Simon Reddy.
Page 72/73: Gulf Side Motel in Cedar Key, Florida; credit Patrick Ward.
Page 74/75: Motel signs in Pigeon Forge, Tennessee; credit Galen Rowell.
Page 76/77: Hobo Inn Motel in Elbe, Washington; credit Wolfgang Kaehler.
Page 78/79: Lobby of the Cold Spring Motel in Plymouth, Massachusetts; credit Kevin Fleming.
Page 80/81: Sign for the Uranium Motel in Utah; credit Joel W. Rogers.
Page 82/83: Sign for the Lake View Café and Motel in Garden City, Utah; credit Scott T. Smith.
Page 84/85: Peg Leg Motel in Rockport, Massachusetts; credit Kevin Fleming.
Page 86/87: Gold Rush Inn in Whitehorse, Yukon Territory; credit Gunter Marx.
Page 88/89: Town Motel in Gardiner, Montana; credit Darrell Gulin.
Page 90/91: Roxy Place Motel in Beardmore, Ontario; credit Patrick Bennett.
Page 92/93: Swan Hotel in Walt Disney World, Florida; reproduced by permission Travel Ink/Abbie Enock.
Page 94/95: Sign for the Woodland Motel in Dillsboro, North Carolina; credit Owen Franken.
Page 96/97: Budget Inn in Daytona Beach, Florida; credit Patrick Ward.
Page 98/99: Motels in Sacramento, California; credit Nik Wheeler.
Page 100/101: Sign for the Lorraine Motel in Memphis, Tennessee; credit Kevin Fleming.
Page 102/103: Detail of Motel sign; credit Robert Holmes.
Page 104/105: Captain's Bounty Motel in Rockport, Massachusetts; credit Kevin Fleming.
Page 106/107: Motel along historic Route 66; credit Nik Wheeler.

Attributions

Page 8/9: Sarasota slogan, Florida State.
Page 12/13: Anon.
Page 14/15: Anon.
Page 18/19: Ralph Waldo Emerson.
Page 20/21: John Babsome Lane Soule.
Page 22/23: William Cowper.
Page 26/27: Martin Luther King.
Page 28/29: Motel promotional literature.
Page 30/31: West Palm Beach slogan, Florida State.
Page 32/33: Anon.
Page 34/35: '50s Oldsmobile ad.
Page 36/37: Anon.
Page 38/39: David Lloyd George.
Page 40/41: Motel promotional literature.
Page 44/45: John Donne.
Page 46/47: Anon.
Page 48/49: Anon.
Page 50/51: Benjamin Disraeli.
Page 52/53: Eagle Lake title.
Page 54/55: Anon.
Page 56/57: Anon.

Page 58/59: Daytona Beach promotional literature, Florida State.
Page 62/63: Motel promotional literature.
Page 66/67: Santa Fe promotional literature, New Mexico.
Page 68/69: Dolly Parton.
Page 72/73: Florida State slogan.
Page 76/77: Washington State slogan.
Page 78/79: Anon.
Page 80/81: Ebenezer Bryce.
Page 82/83: Anon.
Page 84/85: Anon.
Page 86/87: Title of gold rush song.
Page 88/89: Anon.
Page 90/91: Ontario promotional literature.
Page 92/93: 1952 Budd automobile body advertisement.
Page 94/95: North Forty Resort along Interstate 90 promotional literature.
Page 96/97: Anon.
Page 100/101: Memphis promotional literature, Tennessee State.
Page 102/103: Memphis promotional literature, Tennessee State.
Page 104/105: Anon.
Page 106/107: U. S. Travel Bureau.

Designer: WDA
Editor: Alison Moss
Researcher: Suzie Green

Sourcebooks, Inc.
P.O. Box 4410, Naperville, Illinois 60567-4410
(630) 961-3900
FAX: (630) 961-2168

Printed and bound in Spain by Bookprint, S.L, Barcelona

MQ 10 9 8 7 6 5 4 3 2 1

ISBN: 1-57071-595-5